FROM MY HEART

Sealed and Sent

Patricia Oetting

ISBN: 13-978-1492783558

FLAME TREE ... FLAMBOYANT

Also known as Royal Poinciana.

I sit under this very tree, very often. Its flowers are a striking flame-like scarlet and yellow. Its petals remind me of tongues of fire (ACTS 2:3), even of a burning bush (EXOD 3:2). Oftentimes the petals fall on me and on the ground all around. I feel showered from above as I pray, showered with the LOVE of the ALMIGHTY.

I pray for Gifts of the Holy Spirit, not really for the 'gift of tongues' but more for the Gift of WISDOM. That gift should guide me in all that I do. It is enough. I am grateful indeed.

THANK YOU

from Patricia

I offer my deep and sincere gratitude to the following people for helping me with my life, with this book and with my deep appreciation for all that God has given us:

- To Gail Pearson for all her work, skill, time and patience in putting this book together.
- To Jennie Guastella, who was the first one way back when, to read my writing and give me the courage to continue.
- To Father Steve Easterday, who has been a true friend and faithful guide in leading me closer to the Lord. He prays with me, for me, before and after my trips. He has indeed sustained me in many a weary moment.

I ask the Lord's special blessings on them and all who encouraged me assisted me and prayed for me. God Bless All of You.

I most definitely write from my heart about the wonderful people of Haiti whom I love. Please, dear reader, be a witness with me to their plight and then remember them in prayer. In ways that I do not quite understand, I have had a reader or two speak to me about something that I wrote bringing them closer to God in prayer.

I think that the *Sealed and Sent* part of the title refers to my being sealed in the Lord and sent to others; Haiti and elsewhere. But I am also sent by the Lord to you the reader. Blessings on you as you read these thoughts.

TABLE OF CONTENTS

INSIGHTS BY FR. STEVE EASTERDAY

A "TRULY THANKFUL HEART"

May we show forth God's praise, "not only with our lips but in our lives, by giving up our selves" to God's service. Amen.

That prayer comes from the General Thanksgiving in the Morning Prayer service of the Episcopal <u>Book of Common Prayer</u> and for me, it sums up the life of Patricia Oetting. This prayer also speaks of a "truly thankful heart," which also well describes the broad, embracing smile of my friend Patricia. It has been a great joy for me to walk with her as her spiritual director for four years now, as she is so very open to God and his leading. Truly she embodies the call of Jesus to serve the "least" in the world, knowing that when we serve the poor, we serve Jesus himself (Matthew 25:40).

Patricia also embodies the faith of the 23rd Psalm, as she is willing to go into the "valley of the shadow of death," almost daily, knowing in her heart that her Shepherd leads her. Her journeys in Haiti and Africa and her work with the homeless and those under hospice care, often put her in fearsome situations, but in the midst of those, her conviction that "God is with her" causes her to see the power of the Holy Spirit to save and heal. We are privileged in this book to have a glimpse into the mind and heart of such a faithful servant.

My prayer for the reader of this book is that you will know in your heart that, with Patricia, you are a beloved child of the Almighty, in the blessed company of all faithful people who experience the real presence of Jesus as the Lord and Savior of our lives.

Fr. Steve Easterday, Co-Rector, Holy Trinity Episcopal Church, Melbourne, Florida

INSIGHTS BY MEGAN McKENNA

MEDITATIONS STRONGER THAN A RETREAT

Haiti…a land of hope and heartbreak, of hospitality and make-shift homes and hospitals, of gentle and strong people who sing and walk through life, that often-times seems to drag them through devastating weather and disasters that shatter their lives and their dreams. And yet they survive and more than survive, they dig down deep into their spirits and their souls as a people to rise up again and again, to share their daily bread and dreams, often with grace!

Haiti is the poorest nation in the western hemisphere and nearly the smallest but perhaps one of the fiercest and loving of life. Today and in these past years they are seeking to rebuild whole cities, houses, infrastructures, education and health-care systems and their daily lives beyond survival. This is a day to day endurance in seeking the basic necessities of water, food, shelter and medical care.

Haiti's situation and problems can be overwhelming but it is the people; men, women and children, the elderly and sick who are barely surviving in their struggle to live who wrench our hearts, overturn our expectations and stir our souls. They become teachers, wise ones and open doors for everyone, everywhere—to the usually hidden presence of God and all that is holy in our midst. Haiti and those who visit there tell us the truth about our world and reveal to us the depth of our faith and commitment to God's Good News to the Poor. Patricia, in this small book, FROM MY HEART—SEALED AND SENT is a collection of reflections made during and after her many visits to Haiti, captures a tiny sliver of what life is like there and the immense impact that even a short visit can do to one's body, heart and soul. Her meditations are stronger than a retreat or seeing what things appear to be like on the news or in a book. And just as Haiti keeps drawing her back again and again, her words keep drawing us back again and again to the core issues of our faith, our hope and our call to 'love one another as I have loved you' (John 13:34).

Patricia goes to be with the people, especially the least, the youngest and most vulnerable ones. She goes to be with those just born and struggling to hang on to a slender thread of life. These weakest among us often fail and slip away before they have a chance to live 'life ever more abundantly'. We are all offered this 'chance' in our birth and daily thereafter. Her experiences are gut and soul wrenching and her writing is a way of absorbing them and living with them since, in reality, she can do so very little about the situations she visits. But in the true sense of what it means to be a missionary, it is her presence and their presence that is the gift and the power that is exchanged and shared.

In this small book, she seeks to pass on the suffering, the wisdom, the faith and the love that she has known and touched in her time there. They live now in her life. And each reflection is like an arrow to the heart, searing the mind and demanding that we respond with our heart and soul, if only in prayer, or in awareness that we stay with and ponder and hopefully that is expressed in some sort of shared response to make others aware. Then, together we can remember that we are called to do something of our own work of mercy in our life, or in helping those who go to Haiti and share what they can.

This book FROM MY HEART—SEALED AND SENT is actually about community and communion that we all share as The Body of Christ and the liturgy of life, death, resurrection and the presence of the Spirit of the Risen Lord in the Glory of God that draws us all together. What we do in church when we gather to pray is the impetus to get us out of church and into the world—out there—and then return with all that weary and wondrous world in our hearts in communion and solidarity. We can't all go to Haiti, but this book can bring some of Haiti's holiness and harshness and happiness to us. These words are a glimpse of The Other Eucharist (as Dom Helder Camara named it—the living body and blood of Christ with us today). It is a gift to cherish and to share with others in your life while reminding us to be thankful for the goodness of our own lives. These words will break your heart and hopefully break your heart open to the wideness of God's presence and love among us— here at home and in Haiti

---

Ms. McKenna and Patricia have known each other since September 2, 1964, Ms. McKenna is a Roman Catholic storytelling theologian who travels the world speaking to other religious leaders and laypeople.

INSIGHTS BY BARRY MOSER

WE ALL SEARCH FOR MEANING

We all search for meaning. Most of us seldom find it. In Patricia Oetting's memoirs I come as close to finding meaning as I do anywhere else. The ecclesiastical architecture of Chartres or Canterbury does that for me, as does the music of Bach and Pärt and Mozart, and Monteverdi. Ahh, now *that* list is long, very long. I think it was John Updike who said that if it were not for music, he'd be an atheist. I'm not far behind that sentiment, whoever said it, save that I have Oetting and he didn't. Her letters to me about her work in Haiti, San Salvador, & Africa, and her work with the homeless men near where she lives in Florida are, for me, the best and most heart-felt missives about God and the power of Faith that I know. And for that I truly and deeply thank her. It's good for an old reprobate skeptic like me to read these things.

Oetting writes so vividly about her Haitian experiences that I sometimes feel as if I had been there with her. Her stories are raw, tactile, visceral, visually sensual, and deeply, deeply moving. And they are embarrassingly informative to those of us who bask in our daily comforts and whine when some small contrivance of convenience goes on the fritz or the batteries give out or our steak or shrimps are overcooked. The stories she tells are lessons in humility, compassion, and empathy. And when I read (as I did back in the spring of 2010) that some ultra-right wing "conservatives" question the veracity and value of empathy it makes me want to scream. It makes me want to puke. The failure of empathy is our modern world's greatest and deadliest sin. Was it not the failure of world-wide empathy that fomented the heinous deaths of ten to eleven million European Jews, Romani, prisoners of war, and homosexuals in the 1930's and '40's?

I wrote Patricia a letter a few years ago telling her that I had given a talk about Mary Shelley's novel *Frankenstein: Or the Modern Prometheus*. In that talk I said: "I discovered, in my more mature readings of the novel, that it is, for me, a metaphor for the moral transgressions of the twentieth century: namely, the failure of compassion, the demise of manners and civility, the reticence to communicate, the pervasive & malignant presence of racism and bigotry, and the loss of our collective ability to empathize." I reminded her that Tolstoy was of the opinion that the activity of art is based in the "capacity of man to receive another man's expression of feelings and experience those feelings himself." Take that Glenn Beck, Rush Limbaugh. This woman's lessons in humility, compassion, and empathy are important lessons that we should all try to learn from her. Learn from the Christian, selfless examples she sets, as when, in a video about the burying of the Haitian dead, she briefly appears, identified only as "Patricia, the woman from Florida who donates body bags." Yes, she does donate body bags. Body bags bought and paid for with money out of her own pocket. But she does more, far more: she goes to Haiti, at her own expense mind you, and helps load those heavy-duty body bags with the unidentified corpses of dead children and dead adults. She puts herself at risk—financially, emotionally, spiritually, and physically—to help others, many of whom die having no known name, and she does so with no expectation of material reward, nor even an expectation of any kind of recognition, no matter how humble or ephemeral, for what she does.

She sits with the dying. She buries the dead. She offers hope and sympathy. She holds people close, in her arms, in her heart, and in her daily prayers. But her mightiest prayer, the one that surely has the ear of the Creator, is her work. It is her compassion. It is her devotion, her determination, and her loving heart. What follows is evidence.

Barry Moser is a celebrated artist. Some of his most celebrated work has been his illustrations for Lewis Carroll's Alice's Adventures in Wonderland and Through the Looking-Glass. He has illustrated nearly 200 other works, including The Bible and Moby-Dick. His works have been displayed in such places as the British Museum, the Metropolitan Museum, Harvard and the Library of Congress.

Chapter 1

MY FIRST HAITIAN EXPERIENCE

I have just returned from my first trip to Haiti. I have just returned from a place of natural beauty that makes me cry out "WOW

I have just returned from a place that is consumed with poverty and suffering and that makes me cry out "WHY?"

I have just returned from a place that has some very wealthy people who apparently have visual and auditory problems, for they are unable to see or hear the cry of the poor. Perhaps I should say that only part of me has returned, for the part of me that is trying to make some sense of this utter contradiction has remained in HAITI. I remember hearing a Jewish story that I can only recall in part. Upon witnessing great suffering of innocent people, a man cried out to the "All Powerful One", saying, "How can you allow this to be?" "Why don't you do something?" The ALL Powerful One replied, "I did, I sent You" Now trying to relate to that concept of the ALL Powerful One sending me is a bit daunting indeed! Fortunately, there are many of us who have heard the CRY OF THE POOR and have felt compelled by SOMEONE. "You who have been sent", can be interpreted in the plural sense. Thankfully, I am not alone in this mission. The individual YOU, is now a plural one!!

A friend, who has been to Haiti before, states that it seems we are putting a "band-aid" on a hemorrhaging wound. We are not embarrassed to make that feeble attempt. B a n d -aids come in so many different sizes. Surely, if enough of us (this plural YOU) have been sent, and place our band-aids together, the bleeding might stop. Then, when the acute condition has been temporarily stopped, it will be our mission to do something about what caused it to bleed in the first place.

CHAPTER 2

LISTEN TO THE SOUNDS OF HAITI

Hello Haiti my dear friend: just a tease on a hit of Simon and Garfunkel of years ago, the Sounds of Silence. I concentrate now on the sounds that I do hear, not silence. The busy airport terminal where we land is a bit more modern, at least the part that is rebuilt.

We do not have to use movable steps from the plane and walk outdoors to the terminal. We have a tunnel passage like other large airports for these 767 planes. I hear the familiar sounds of the band before I see it. Glad to tip you guys and thanks for putting me in the mood of the Caribbean. I hear an even more welcome sound.

"Hello, Patricia". Three of Mother Teresa's Missionaries of Charity sisters were apparently on the same flight. One knows me. In three weeks I shall return to Haiti and spend one month at their convent compound in Port au Prince, holding babies, loving babies, and helping with some clinics. My heart already begins to be happy!

As we head for the Coconut Villa Hotel I am pleased to hear the sounds of big trucks. Heavy equipment types for the clearing of rubble, still to be seen in many places, and for the construction, repair and rebuilding that is so needed. Motorbikes zooming by and loud horns from impatient drivers are familiar sounds. The roads seem to have more pot holes. The streets are still lined with 'tent cities',
apparently put up on any empty
lot or spot. These tents have
now been here for many, many
months and are showing the wear
of the bright sun, the wind, and
the rain. Duct tape, blue tarp and
pieces of corrugated metal seem
to help some of them. In other
places it is not quite holding these
temporary homes together. Despite

pieces of rope and less than sturdy poles these 'homes' are sagging, and sadly sagging. Hurricane season starts in a few weeks. These tents are all so very close together.   I am sure sounds travel quickly from one to another. Crying babies and laughing children must blend with shouts of anger and impatience and spread to the tents nearby.

In one area I see some colorful, sturdy looking, one large room type houses being built by the government. I wonder just who shall be chosen to live in them, how long it takes to build them, and where

others will be built.   Many of the tents are on private land. The sounds of these many questions run through my mind. What kind of questions are running through the mind of these poor tent dwellers".   Do they think, do they pray,   "How long, Oh Lord, how long?"

Sounds change quickly as we reach our hotel, still protected by that guard out front holding a rifle.   Birds are singing in the lush flowering trees of this little oasis.

The welcoming words of the staff at the registration desk greet us.   Many of us are familiar faces now. A quick visit to our rooms to drop off our personal luggage and to freshen up, then off we go in the van with the rest of the luggage piled high on top.   Medicines, medical instruments and more supplies are on their way to Mission Ranch Clinic in Cite Soleil. This community is the largest and still most dangerous slum in the Western Hemisphere.   Weapon carrying gang members w h o h a v e escaped from the prison have returned home.   We cannot currently use a wider street along the garbage filled canal for easier access to our clinic. These gang members seem to shoot randomly and throw heavy bricks.   Our driver has to use the narrow, winding streets, which sometimes requires an almost ninety degree turn.   He knows his stuff and we do well.

The United Nations troops are making many trips past our clinic in a big tank and on foot. We are safe and unafraid.

After we set up our treatment areas and re-stock the pharmacy we head back to the hotel for rest and cool drinks. Most of us have been awake since 3 a.m. and have driven to Miami for our almost two hour flight. The swimming pool is enjoyed by some. We share dinner and laughter. We get to know each other, many of whom we are meeting for the first time. We head to bed, but sleep did not come as expected!

It seems that a Disco Club has opened right next door to this secluded villa. The most enthusiastic, live disc jockey started at 9 p.m. and continued until 3 a.m. Loud speakers ensure that the entire neighborhood can hear every note. The music itself is not the problem, just its volume. I am sure that hearing loss will result over time from these decibels of sound. I could almost feel the vibration. The window next to my bed did shake at times. These songs were not lullabies or even a slow and mellow ballad. I realized this place is for the young and the young at heart. I know that I am definitely n o t young, and have just learned that I am not very young at heart r i g h t now! I must be old in body and in spirit. I needed more than the three and one half hours of sleep I got before t h e rooster awakened me. I wonder if the noise also disrupts his lifestyle. Was that a bit more of a grumpy cock-a-doodle-do?

During the hours of wakefulness I had much to think about. I wondered if the sounds of that music were welcomed by all in the tents right down the street. Did they consider it free entertainment? What did they think of that song, 'I LOVE MY LIFE', with its repetitive lyrics? Did they truly like to hear that over and over? Did they love the situation that they were in? Did even those in the Disco really LOVE it? Was it only a brief respite from a life of instability?

On Easter Sunday this year I was at a beautiful sunrise service at the water's edge of a retreat house. An instrumental song filled me with emotional and spiritual awakening as we passed from the sorrow of Good Friday through to the joyous celebration of our Risen Savior. We exalted in the Resurrection. We felt HOPE for the future. I knew nothing at all about the piece of music, I only knew I felt comforted and at peace. As I lay there awake in Haiti, I wished that I could somehow play this music for the finale. Give the people in hot, crowded tents and dilapidated hovels that they must call home, a bit of comforting HOPE. Perhaps they would feel what I experienced through it.

When I later asked the name of that piece of music, I was surprised to hear it was from an opera by Puccini, TURANDOT, The name of it was NESSUN DORMA which in English means NO ONE SLEEP!! I did not know that the piece was part of a Persian fairy tale. I learned that the answer to the song I loved so much that fills EACH NIGHT AND DIES EACH DAY is HOPE

Imagine that I was uplifted, and they sang about HOPE dying in the day! Fortunately, as most fairy tales give witness, this opera ends with jubilation. You see there was another riddle, a final one. The answer to it is "ITS NAME IS LOVE". HOPE was definitely not *only* possible, it was alive!

Perhaps these wonderful Haitian people were living the first riddle, awakening each morning to the wondering if HOPE was possible. I still would like to play that musical operatic aria for them. I pray that when I come into Haiti, alone or with my wonderful Haiti clinic team, we bring them HOPE. First and foremost HOPE. The medicines, teaching, caring, all wrapped in HOPE. I pray that I can help— that we can help-- bring them a better life, a healthier and productive life as they live in a rebuilt and flourishing land with green, tree-filled mountains, and a self-sustaining economy once again. May that HOPE be as the new water tank outside the clinic: water that is clean, safe from disease, accessible and free. This trip we treated 720 people in two days, and 65 teeth were removed. Our added sounds were deep and grateful sighs and some yawns.

May Haiti be filled with HOPE...be filled with LOVE....which was the final answer in the opera. I cannot wait to return for my next trip in three short weeks. The last sounds I now dwell on are gratitude for all I have and intercession for all of the Haitian people. Please LORD, listen to their SOUNDS OF SILENCE, their n i g h t time prayer and do keep HOPE alive for them.

Chapter 3

JUST NOT SURE

When I return from my frequent trips to Haiti I am often asked the question, "Do you see any improvement there"? That question is often followed by: "What did they do with all the money"?

Well, my response to the second question is that I have no idea. I do not know if they even got the money; nor do I know who "they" are! I now concentrate more on that first question, particularly the first few words; "Do I see", **"Do I see?"** As I disembark from the plane, entering Haiti once again.

I do see a somewhat improved airport, except for that congested, unorganized baggage pick up area. It seems like a foretelling of what a congested and really unorganized Haiti might be like. The area outside the airport is sad.

First you pass tent cities on the left, tent cities on the right. I do not need to

mention the people who are always interceding: needy people begging for help along the way. That is the same as I have always experienced.

When we drive past the Presidential Palace we see that it is still in a sorry state.

I do believe that the new President lives on the grounds in a separate building. I wonder though and try to compare that fact with a "what if" scenario.

What if it was the White House in the USA? Would we still have confidence in a leadership that did not quickly repair-quickly restore--.quickly rebuild, first of all the House where so many important decisions are made affecting the people. I seriously doubt that the government of Haiti is waiting until all those who have also had damage to, or lost their homes, are in better straights. I just do not believe that they could be that gracious or compassionate. Of course I could be wrong.

I share with you, that there were actually some of the Haitian people who thought this shaking of the earth happened to everyone, everywhere. They wondered how friends or family had fared during those seconds of terror. Ah, yes, the poor sometimes do have a more global concept of things happening to all of us, at the same time, everywhere. Yes, in a very real way, we are all in this together. I do love that concept, because in my heart of hearts, I do know that it is true.

Then we might drive past the Roman Catholic Cathedral, which is now a shell of its former state. I have been there before the quake. I know its former

beauty. Now it is like a shell, a piece of a shell. Picture the Roman Coliseum, just bits of walls standing. The frames of the stained glass windows now reflect a hollow, empty beauty.

The city roads are still filled with potholes, numerous potholes. I have most definitely felt them in automobiles, vans and motorbike. I assure you that these potholes are numerous! The city streets are depressing to me. They are filled with plastic. Oh, so much plastic; water bottles, soda bottles, even little bags that hold a few ounces of clean water. All of these are just thrown on the street, with nary a care as to where they land or where they remain.

Garbage is everywhere. Pigs and goats, even dogs and cats must be happy. They do not have to search for a meal! Oh, how I wish that there were containers on every street and that they had some way of actually recycling this debris. Oh, and then there is the Styrofoam! All of this, other than being an actual eyesore is a terrible obstruction during the heavy rains that so often occur there. It is a blockage that could so easily be prevented.

I go back now to that earlier question of **"Do I see"**? I concentrate more on an inner vision, a different insight. I do not live far from the Intracoastal Waterway in Florida. I refer particularly to the Indian River, which is just a bit more than one mile away. I drive by this waterway on a daily basis. A few early mornings I looked at it as a sheet of metal. It is still and oh so quiet. One could easily imagine that t h i s was how it always was and that it was just a surface beauty. Ah, yes, one could think 'that was all there was to it' and yet I KNEW it was not. I have been fortunate enough to know the beauty of 'fins and flippers, s e a w e e d and seashells'. All of this and so much more that inhabit the depths beneath the surface. All of this is just hidden from our view. We have to be willing to look deeper.

I go to a more spiritual side and think of the words from St Teresa of Avila, a Saint of old. She cautions: "Within us lies something incomparably more precious than what we see outside ourselves. Let us not imagine that we are hollow inside.

A modern day priest, Fr. Richard Rohr, teaches us about another "kind of something beneath". Yes, these are my words. He states: "Contemplation is radical because it is trying to address the root, the underlying place where illusions and ego are generated. It touches the unconscious, where most of our wounds and our needs for healing lie.

Oh, my, how I feel that need for Haiti. Perhaps Haiti is trying to address wounds and hurts to get to the root of its problem and I just cannot see!

A little while ago I learned a new word. I enjoyed the way it seemed to roll off my tongue. The word is LIMINAL. In a way, I liked the outside of the word itself before I even knew what it meant. The definition made me enjoy it all the more. The definition is: "A threshold barely perceptible belonging to the point of conscious awareness below which something cannot be seen, experienced or felt." It is even described as a point at which a stimulus is great enough to produce an effect. Interestingly, one writer described pregnancy as a way of looking at its meaning. One could never d r e a m o f all the miraculous happenings and changes that are taking place in a pregnant woman's belly. Ah, but they are happening!

I pray and I hope that HAITI is LIMINAL. That it is on a threshold of new beginnings, and that it is simply a matter of not being able to see it with my physical eyes. I use my inner eye, my insight, to help me recall that ever-so still and quiet Indian River, with lots going on beneath. I hope that Haiti realizes the 'something more precious is inside', knowing it is not hollow, and that the outside can be deceiving. I hope it can address its roots and find the wounds that need healing. The people of Haiti are wonderful, and are strong in body and spirit. I know they want a Haiti that once again has forests that can hold back rainwater which now causes mudslides and floods. Maybe the government is planting new trees that the goats will not eat and I just cannot see it. Maybe the government is working on clean, safe water for the entire country, not just areas here and there, and I just cannot see it. Maybe the government is ensuring public schools for all .and making sure that their own people have the necessary equipment and supplies to build many more jobs there. The Haitian people need to have their own jobs, not watch others do the building for them. Maybe roads are being built to connect people and places .and I just do not see them. It seems that everything takes a long time in Haiti. This LIMINAL period might take more time than I realize, yet I sincerely hope that it is happening. I answer that question now, "Do I see" with, "Ah yes", my inner eye, my insight knows that it is making progress; It will just take a while. It is still in the early stages of pregnancy so to speak.

Chapter 4

BLOOD, SWEAT AND TEARS

Two weeks in Haiti have left me physically and emotionally exhausted. Within a few hours of my return, I felt a deep sadness come over me. I wanted to cry. I needed to shed tears. The flight from Port-au-Prince to Miami was uneventful. The much shorter one to Orlando had much turbulence. Beautiful, dense clouds were the cause of many a dip of that plane wing and some stomachs. I was very happy to be home, yet I needed to cry.

I felt like a sponge when I arrived in Haiti. It was raining, which was fittingly appropriate since a wet sponge always absorbs more. The phrase BLOOD, SWEAT, AND TEARS runs through my mind like a somber refrain, as I recall the two weeks of volunteering at the Missionaries of Charity compound. My focus is on the sick babies. There are approximately eighty babies currently in the volunteer house, awaiting the completion of a new shelter in a few weeks. The earthquake of January 2010 did much damage to the old building. We await the rising of the new one with much joy. The babies are so sick; suffering from severe malnutrition, dehydration, worms, diarrhea, malaria, pneumonia, TB, anemia, scabies, and even some severe burns from very hot porridge. Some require feeding tubes, IV fluids, oxygen, nebulizer treatments, powerful antibiotics, and lots of vitamins.

Of course, countless diaper changes are required; upwards of hundreds each day. As I walked from the front gate I passed hundreds of little wet diapers. There had been three days of rain and without sunshine, these diapers could not dry.

The BLOOD SWEAT AND TEARS thought is not of the rock band from the late 1960's, even though one song AND WHEN I DIE, has just popped into my head. Nor do I refer to the words of President Theodore Roosevelt in June 1897 when he addressed the Naval War College, in Newport, RI. He discussed the

nation's triumph because of labor, anguish, blood, sweat, and tears that had been spent. Nor does it refer to Winston Churchill's discussion of how to get through the terrible ordeal of war, forecasting many months of struggle and suffering. He had nothing to offer but blood, toil, tears a n d sweat. Yet perhaps, in a way, it includes all of the above.

The struggle, the suffering of the poorest of the poor Haitian people, with whom I am involved, is indeed a battle of survival. Even the musical group with the great horn section that I previously mentioned, had enough thoughts about death to have that one song become a great hit.

On my last trip there I recall writing a b o u t a woman 'wailing' as she sat by a nearby gate, because her child had just died of severe malnutrition. It was my last memory of that trip.

Now, five months later, on the first morning I wake in Haiti, I am witness to the exact same situation, at the same gate. The 'wail' is always the same to me. I was headed for morning mass at 6:30 a.m. Oh, how I prayed for her, and for everyone whose children had died during the night, in all parts of the world. I prayed for lasting comfort for them. The mother was still sitting on that bench as I returned to my room. I approached her, instinctively pulling her towards me for what I refer to as a 'long, leaning into'. It is not just a psychological leaning on someone. It is much more of a connection of spirit, becoming one with the emotion and allowing more tears to flow. All I could say over and over again was 'MWEM REGRET SA', 'MWEM REGRET SA', I am so sorry. I am so sorry. This mother's child was only eight months old and died of severe malnutrition. How can this keep happening? I spent the day feeding as many as I could, holding them and loving them.

The diapers were still not drying.

I awoke the next morning to the sound of a rooster. Being a 'city girl', growing up in the Bronx and in Newark, all I learned about roosters came from a cartoon or a book. I thought they 'awoke' at dawn, greeted the day with a "cock a doodle d o.", and that was that! In Haiti I learn that free

roaming roosters squawk all night l o n g, and that here it actually sounds like a four syllable "cock a doodle". Last year a few of the volunteers came up

with phrases that we thought sounded like; GET THE LEAD OUT......
MAKE THE COFFEE ...and mine was ...LORD HAVE MERCY. So at
5:30 am, before the sunrise, I prayed with a few squawking roosters. I
laughed thinking it was like the recitation of a psalm refrain from a Sunday
service, only it was a silly one that I just made up. We shall all now recite
the psalm by half verse:

LORD HAVE MERCY
HELP THE SUFFERING

LORD HAVE MERCY
FEED THE HUNGRY

LORD HAVE MERCY
PROVIDE CLEAN WATER

LORD HAVE MERCY
DRY THE DIAPERS

LORD HAVE MERCY
ON US ALL

I spend most of my time with the sickest ones, giving nebulizer treatments,
inserting feeding tubes in those tiny noses, and starting IVs. The SWEAT,
part of the BLOOD, SWEAT, TEARS, refrain is quite real here. It is in the
90's and very humid. We often do not even have a fan since we have
intermittent electricity. I went to visit the older children and as I sat down,
a precious little girl came running to me, sat down on my lap, cuddled and
snuggled into the crook of my arm. She fell asleep almost immediately.
For about an hour she stayed there, leaning on my arm which was almost
asleep. The sweat from her face fell on my arm, the sweat from my face,
fell on her head. Ah, yes, it was one of those "Nowhere else on earth would
I rather be" moments,

A bit later, I w a s checking on the little boy to whom I had been giving
the nebulizer treatments. His breathing definitely did not look good, despite
the oxygen, the IV's and potent antibiotics. I thought he would die soon. I
was a few cribs away feeding a hungry little girl who was so very eager for
each spoonful. A woman had approached his crib and I was glad he was not
alone. I thought perhaps it w as his mother. Then I heard the 'w a i l', and
I knew he had slipped into eternity. I went to him, to say a prayer and kiss
him goodbye. I then returned to the feeding of the hungry little girl. I had
to take care of the living. The woman had run out through the screen door.

I went outside and saw her sitting on the bench by the gate. This is the same gate where I seem to always be comforting a woman. She was his aunt. His mom and dad live a few towns away and she already has a two month old baby. We discuss the burial and then I just sit real close with her, sharing touch, presence, tissues and tears.

Yes, I also cry.

The next day, at the time after lunch, when we are to 'rest' a bit, I hear another 'wail', and then many other voices. I am not sure about those other voices. I look down from my balcony and see (Yes, at that same bench, by the same gate) another woman, surrounded by many of the attendants who care for the babies. In another area I see a 'worker' all alone and sobbing. I find out that a ten year old girl had been ill for a while. All the workers knew and loved her. Her mother had stayed with her here, leaving her two other children hours away with relatives. The little one was in and out of local hospitals. She finally had surgery, and had died some hours after it. So, this grief was most palpable, shared by many. Since the mother had support at that time, I went to the lone worker. I sat next to her, and hugged her. Yes, another 'leaning into'. After a while I went to the mother. Fr Rick would bury her beloved child, and she was comforted by that thought.

The BLOOD part of that phrase, B L O O D , SWEAT AND TEARS is a bit different than that of Churchill or Roosevelt. I have been a nurse for many, many years, working in the ER for seventeen years and in Out Patient Surgery for eleven years. I have started countless IV's and consider myself 'good' at it! Well, that was all before Haiti, all before dehydrated and malnourished babies who had barely a vein to find. I was inserting a needle into a 'thread' that I could barely feel. I always have depended on the feel not the sight, needing the bounce of the vein. Last year I did not always succeed. But this time, by the grace of God, I was able to get each one started with only one stick. What a blessing for me to see that bit of BLOOD return in the catheter, and to realize 'I was in'. I was never so happy to see blood in my life.

I related all this to my spiritual director, Father Steve. I shared how I had felt; for some reason this trip was to comfort all these women who needed me. He and I talked about Jesus. I remarked that when I think of HIM alone in the Garden before the crucifixion, I wish I could wipe HIS tears. There is a poem written in 1845 called *CHRIST IN THE GARDEN*.

It said in part,

"SO DEEP WAS HIS SORROW,
SO FERVENT HIS PRAYER,
THAT DOWN O'ER HIS BOSOM,
ROLLED BLOOD, SWEAT and TEARS"

Father Steve reminded me and assured m e that the tears I wiped were indeed
the tears of Jesus.   I am grateful for that opportunity.   I felt like a
sponge that had absorbed much, now I am wrung out, dried out.   The sad
mood and need to cry were part of the wringing, I am sure.   At the end of
Churchill's speech he asked: "What is our aim?" VICTORY, VICTORY at
all costs, in spite of all terror, however hard and long the road may be. As a
Christian, I believe we shall have our ultimate victory .in Jesus. Perhaps I
can now sing 'VICTORY IN JESUS' as the recurring mantra. Let the
BLOOD,SWEAT and TEARS be just a necessary part of that by which I am
humbled. Honored and blessed to be able to do for the poorest of the
poor, I look forward to my next visit and all that I shall learn.

Chapter 5

I NEED TO SIT WITH WISDOM

The Scripture reading of Wisdom 6:12-16 in the Roman Catholic Bible seemed rather appropriate today.

"WISDOM HASTENS TO MAKE HERSELF KNOWN IN ANTICIPATION OF THEIR DESIRE. WHOEVER WATCHES FOR HER AT DAWN SHALL NOT BE DISAPPOINTED, FOR HE SHALL FIND HER SITTING BY HIS GATE".

I really like that vision of WISDOM, not disappointing, and waiting, not in any hurry to leave, perhaps waiting for me. I need to sit with WISDOM. Our bedroom is less than one hundred feet from a locked gate with barbed wire atop for protection. I see a mother there, right now. I hear a mother there, right now. She wails in a sorrowful lament for her child, her baby boy has just died. She sits with other women whose babies are also very ill. Do they wonder if their child might also not survive? Oh, WISDOM, please be with them. Do not disappoint them.

I would like to go down there and comfort her. I am not sure if she speaks English and my Creole is limited. I think that she needs to be with these women who know her sorrow, who know how to comfort her in ways that I cannot. Sadly this is an all too familiar situation for the women of Haiti. Her little boy was the last one I had helped Sister with last evening, I can see his face and his body; a body that could give you a wrong impression on first glance, almost looking chubby and healthy. But he had a severe edema. He was very swollen with fluid from another form of malnutrition. We are so much more used to seeing the malnutrition that presents with a wasting away, with sparrow-like extremities, with folds of skin hanging down, and a saddened, gaunt face staring out at us. This little boy had severe vomiting, diarrhea, and that was complicated by pneumonia. Had he survived the pneumonia we would have treated the malnutrition and he eventually would have many folds of skin hanging down, just like the little boy two cribs away, whose dark skin has pulled away, peeled away, from much of his face, torso and legs, leaving a sharp contrast of color with the almost raw pink flesh. This tiny boy is getting stronger. He hangs on to the edge of the crib and sways back and forth to the music that we play. We all smile and laugh as he entertains us. The workers, the volunteers, even the Sisters, dance in the narrow space between cribs to accompany him. We encourage his exercise. We feel HOPE.

The little one who has just died must be dancing with the LORD OF THE DANCE in heaven. He is safe, not sick, not hungry, and shall be with the Lord for today, tomorrow, and all of eternity, in a newly restored body. I am rather frustrated, tearfully so, trying to understand how things work, or do NOT work here in Haiti. Yesterday morning Sister had given this mother the fare to take her son to a hospital about one hour away on a tap tap (the colorfully painted trucks used as taxis). For some reason that hospital did not keep the baby, thinking he belonged elsewhere. The second hospital she went to, much closer to us, also did not keep him. She came back to the Sisters of course. In a way, we did not keep him either, since he is now in heaven.

The Scripture reading of today continued:

'FOR TAKING THOUGHT OF WISDOM IS THE PERFECTION OF PRUDENCE AND WHOEVER, FOR HER SAKE KEEPS VIGIL, SHALL QUICKLY BE FREE FROM CARE.

I really must work on that keeping vigil with WISDOM, sitting at a gate and spending lots of time with her. I would like to be free from care, if only for a very brief time during my stay here in Haiti. I have much to learn. I think that POVERTY has taken such a hold on these desperate people that they have rules of their own. The prudent thing for me, as an outsider here in Haiti, is just to be careful in making quick judgments. Ah yes, I have much to learn from WISDOM.

I headed downstairs, two flights of uneven, winding, concrete stairs to pour some medications a bit early. There are thirty one stairs to be exact. It is Sunday, and the daily routine is altered. A children's mass is being offered. I had gone to the 6:30 am, mass in the chapel with the Sisters. At the foot of the stairs I saw the mother whose baby had died stretched out on a very narrow bench, facing the concrete wall. I was surprised that no one was with her now, or even around. I sat down, near her head and lightly touched her back so that she would know that she was not alone. I saw tears roll down her cheeks. Tears also ran down mine. We shared the silence and tissues. She was exhausted. I could feel it and see it. I felt privileged to be able to spend some time with her. I was happy that she could actually get some rest, some sleep. I worried that she might hear a baby crying, and awake, looking for her son, forgetting that he had died. It was only three hours since he had died. I recalled the words of my spiritual director, Father Steve. I had said I was not really sure exactly what my ministry was. He assured me that it was one of MY PRESENCE AND MY PRAYER. I could pray with this woman and was honored to be present with her. I am sure that some people passing by wondered about this old, gray haired white woman sitting in that narrow space with a sleeping woman. School children ran by after mass, headed for the courtyard to play. Other mothers played with their babies. At noon, after I was there for two and a half hours, her mother came for her. She had been sharing the news with family and all decided that the Sisters could take care of the burial arrangements. Very few Haitian people can afford to bury their loved ones, even a baby. The workers got them both something to eat and drink, and they left. I went down to the babies. I felt a touch of sadness as I walked by that empty crib. But, he was in heaven. His mom was with her family and I prayed that WISDOM would be with us all.

I rested a bit during the afternoon break and went back to the babies at 3 p.m. Another little boy was in that crib. Soon I realized that the workers were being told that the Sisters' driver was up at the gate. I knew that it had to be to transport that little body to the morgue. I quickly decided that I would accompany him. I had the privilege of sitting with the mother, and now I would be with her son's body. And so I did, I knew that Father Rick and his team would pray for him and bury him on Thursday. I have done many a burial with Fr Rick and knew that it would be done with love and dignity.

Ah, WISDOM, thank you for indeed 'ANTICIPATING MY DESIRE' to be present and prayerful to both mother and her little boy who I tried to help in illness and in death. Thank you for meeting me with solicitude and comfort. A Please, dear WISDOM, when the mother looks for comfort, may she find you sitting at the gate of her soul. Thank you........... AMEN... AMEN

Chapter 6

LEARNING TO STRETCH

 It was in Haiti, Port-au-Prince, Haiti exactly, before the earth there slid, shook, and the people quaked. It was not a solitary, one-time experience, a suddenly overwhelming moment like Thomas Merton had, not one specific, never to be forgotten moment. It was a compilation of the moments of direct eye contact, and the BEING there, the being right THERE, in the midst of the poorest of the poor, amidst the throngs!

When I am in Haiti I look at the vast sea of humanity and I feel helpless. I so much want to hold all of them in my heart, for I cannot hold them in my hands. In reading St. Augustine I realize I can indeed stretch my heart to hold them all.

He says, "Suppose you are going to fill some holder or container and you know you will be given a large amount. Then you set about stretching your sack or wineskin, or whatever it is. Why? Because you know the quantity you have to put into it is great and your eyes tell you there is not enough room. By stretching it you increase the capacity of the sack. This is how God deals with us. (Tract 4 pl 35).

Taking in all of this suffering of the poorest of the poor is no easy task. I often need to withdraw to a quiet place, concentrate on the immensity and intensity of the Lord. I also stretch my spirit to take in as much of the Lord as I can hold. Then, fed and nourished, I can once again deal with the throngs of that pressing humanity, one by one and person to person.

I go through a marketplace on the way in and out of a clinic at St. Joseph church and school. It is an unreal experience. The road, or what should be a road, has been thoroughly encroached upon by people and the products they have to sell. Large painted trucks, once used as 'tap taps' (where people would tap on the driver's window to get off) were now being used for people to sit under, crouch under, lie under to avoid the hot sun, all the while selling whatever they can.

Others try to make their way down this congested road with wheelbarrows loaded to the top, and with carts that seem like only an ox could pull.

And yet, I see a man almost doubled over straining to push a weight that seems utterly impossible. Now getting through this mass of humanity in a van takes time. In the slow crawl of my transportation I manage to make direct eye contact with the people. I pray that they can, in some mysterious way sense the compassion I feel!!!

I do many different things when I am in Haiti. I have held babies, lovingly, until they have died. I have dispensed medication for those with worm infestations, a fever, malnutrition or chronic cough. I have squeezed pus out of abscesses and changed dressings of non-healing wounds. I have  buried the abandoned dead with a wonderful Catholic priest, before the quake. I have been privileged to enter into the PAIN, the SUFFERING, the HURT, of the people, as I have learned to feel the COMPASSION of Jesus.

All this, was my Epiphany, my moment in God's time: A moment that can only be expressed as 'THERE IS NO WHERE ELSE ON GOD'S EARTH THAT I WOULD RATHER BE'. It was then and it is still………

Chapter 7

PONDERING THE PIETA

You were wearing a bright pink outfit. Your little body was burning up with fever. I even used pink washcloths as cool compresses to soothe you.

Baby powder, a clean diaper and a brand new white smock now cover your little body. I have dressed you in your burial clothes. You were so sick that your parents brought you here to the Sisters and left you. They did not stay with you, nor did they ever return.

I have spent the last four and one half hours of your life intimately connected with you. Your eyes were open when first we met and I know that when we looked at each other our souls felt the connection. Should I be fooling myself on that account? I do know that you could feel my attention and my presence. I sang to you. I prayed for you. I blessed you with holy water. I kept "in touch" with you all the time, stroking your little body and holding you.

Bedsides of the dying are familiar places for me as a Hospice Volunteer. But oh, this is not the same at all! The aide takes your body that I have gently wrapped in a cloth down to the morgue. I take leave, in tears, to get a cup of tea and finish packing for my trip home to Florida.

This trip will soon end. This little girl was the second one this week I had become ever so connected with before her death. She was ten months old. This other baby was six months old and only weighed four pounds. I held her in the crook of my arm. It was like holding a tiny sparrow with its rapidly beating heart. I only held her for two and a half hours. Her story was even sadder. Her mother had literally thrown her away after giving birth. Another woman picked her up and has lovingly cared for her since then. Dear Lord, please bless that woman and help the woman who discarded her child.

These are just two seemingly insignificant lives. They are two out of the many, many who die each day. People ask me why I go to Haiti. I often ask myself the same question. Do I really think I make a difference? Mother Teresa said that what her Missionaries of Charity did was like adding a drop of water to the ocean---but it was still a drop. As far as the magnitude of suffering that these poorest of the poor endure, I do very little to improve it. I believe, though, that I did make a difference for those two little baby girls who were loved by me until the end of their lives.

Other babies will get better with all the medications, IVs, nourishing food and vitamins provided by the Sisters. Interactions with volunteers assist in that healing. Last week a group of five came while I was there. I met a man in his 50's without arms. He was scooting around in his wheelchair using his feet. I sat next to him in a rocking chair with a little baby boy in my lap. I watched as he managed to loosen the sock on his right foot with his left foot. The little boy's bare foot touched h i s foot and I was beyond words as I watched them play, "This little piggy went to market.....this little piggy stayed home".

I could barely hold back the tears when he told me that he felt so badly because he knew the babies wanted to be picked up and there was no way he could do it. Dear God in heaven, I do not even have the words to tell you how I feel about all this. Please, please help him. I am on the outside looking at his willing, generous spirit and his hurting heart.

I find the rocker to be soothing for me also. I often think of the Blessed Mother who had learned to "ponder" .....to ponder things in her heart. I recall how the Greek word actually meant to "turn over and over and over again". To me it seems like rocking. I actually bought a knick-knack of a small rocking chair that I keep next to a statue of Mary, to remind me that pondering is necessary. Answers do not come quickly, if at all. Maybe I shall be pondering for a long, long time. Maybe I shall have the answers that make sense to people who ask me why I go to Haiti, or to myself. Maybe not.

I think of Mary once again. I think of her after the death of her son. I see the Pieta by Michelangelo in my mind's eye --pure white marble. But that soon changed in my mind to my idea of how she would look like at Calvary. I picture a woman sitting in the dirt under the cross. I picture a woman cradling her son's body with his matted hair and dried blood all over. I picture a woman touching the puncture wounds that ripped open more as they removed the nails from his body....and that large hole in his side. I picture a woman who stood under the cross so that she could understand the cross. I picture a woman who must ponder some more.

Help me, dear mother Mary. Help me. I have so much to learn...so much to ponder in my heart......

Chapter 8

MYSTERY AND A MATTER OF FACT

Oftentimes, I have heard and I have even used the expression, "I shall never forget this as long as I live". Well, this has to be at the top of unforgettable experiences for me.

It was in Haiti, It was on a Tuesday in June. I had awakened at dawn's light to the sounds of babies crying and a rooster crowing. A very large black pig that lives next door just slept on. I actually smiled when I read the Scripture for the day. Matthew 6: 7... "Do not throw pearls before swine lest they trample them under foot and turn and tear you to pieces". It seems that even a

nudge, never mind a shove, would be more than she could do at the present moment.

I was reading my PRACTICE OF THE PRESENCE OF GOD, expecting to learn what Brother Lawrence could teach me about relationship and experience of the Creator. The message in the foreword seemed to grab my attention. "The harried citizen is pulled one way by mystery and the other way by matter of fact". The commentator wrote that in 1941, before I was born, about a situation that even existed in 1666. As I write this I realize it was a summary of the day that will live in my memory. Ah yes, mystery and matter of fact combined.

A little boy named Christopher, two months old and weighing only six and a half pounds, was very ill. His mother had died at his birth. He was delivered by C-Section and I presume he was premature. His abdomen was grossly distended, His breathing was labored, made worse I am sure, by that large belly pushing on his diaphragm. The stomach contents, which were returned after insertion of a nasogastric tube, led us to believe he had an intestinal obstruction. Christopher needed more help than we could give him at Mother Teresa's Missionaries of Charity facility. Another baby had just arrived who was in trouble from severe malnutrition. She also needed help that would best be treated at St Damien's Hospital. My friend, Fr Rick, priest and physician, had started the hospital. The hospital was about thirty minutes away. (I had emailed Fr Rick a few weeks before to let him know I would be in Haiti for one month, but we had not yet been in contact with each other this trip.)

The sisters' driver was ready for transport. I wrapped my little Christopher in a blanket for comfort and grabbed an extra tiny diaper "just in case". His grandmother, now his only mother, was with me. We headed for help with the other little sick girl and her mother. The only thing missing was a portable oxygen cylinder. We did not have one.

The traffic, as usual, was heavy, noisy and congested as we drove along the Port-au-Prince streets. If there is a designated pattern to this traffic, I have yet to discover it.

 The windows were rolled down since we did not have air conditioning. I cradled little Christopher in my arms. His grandmother sat behind the driver and the mom and little girl were behind me. I always feel honored to be riding in a vehicle that has Missionaries of Charity so boldly written on it. I am sure that all easily recognize the Sisters' vehicles. Not too long into our journey, little Christopher died in my arms. It was not difficult for him. He just slowly slipped into eternity. It was most definitely difficult for me. Oh how I yelled at the Holy Spirit in silent prayer. You might not think that is possible to silently yell, but I assure you it is. I screamed in my distress to the Holy Spirit, without giving the slightest indication to anyone in the vehicle. No one knew but me. Oh how I shouted for help not to shed a tear. I knew that I could not do that on my own. I am just about in tears now as I write this. Oh how I begged for assistance. I was sure if I let on what had happened that his grandmother would start wailing and the other mother would think maybe her baby would also die...and Lord knew what the driver would do. I had to remain calm...had to pretend that all was as it had been. We arrived at an intersection with an actual traffic light! These traffic lights are few and far between for me. In the middle of traffic a young boy was begging for money. He approached my open window, saw the

blanket and wanted me to show him the baby. Oh dear God, how I prayed for that light to change quickly. How could I show him my little dead Christopher and not shed a tear? I yelled again, silently, at the Holy Spirit. I cannot do this alone ....help me! Now, I must confess that I have never, ever, yelled at the Holy Spirit before. This was a desperate situation and I needed help. I feared that I would soon 'lose it'. And then, loud and clear, resounding through the noisy streets of Haiti, I heard, "GOD BLESS PATRICIA. GOD BLESS PATRICIA. GOD BLESS PATRICIA." three times.

I thought that I must have hallucinated I thought how could this be? I looked out that open window, and there, right next to me, on the back of a motorbike was Fr Rick, shouting out to all of Haiti. GOD BLESS PATRICIA. I barely had time to say that I was headed toward his hospital. He rode off, out of my sight.   He was there and then he was not.   Oh, but it was 'all that I needed'. The Holy Spirit came through for me in a way that I never would have dreamed ...I knew I could make it ....I could pretend all was the same until I got to the hospital. It was as if I had a mountaintop experience, a transformation on the mountain, even though I was on flat ground in the busy city. My hearing of GOD BLESS PATRICIA was like what Jesus must have felt at the Transfiguration when He heard: "This is .my beloved son in whom I am well pleased".   That message was the same for me on that Tuesday in June in Haiti, the island of mountains. When we arrived at the hospital Fr Rick had apparently called ahead.   I had an English speaking person greet me as I entered.   All went well as I proceeded into the Emergency Room and told them the truth of what had happened.   The physician pronounced him dead, and spoke to his grandmother; this poor woman who had now lost her grandson as well as her daughter.   A bootie had fallen from his tiny foot.   I gave it to her as we cried together in a warm hug. We were told Father Rick would offer mass in the morning for our little Christopher and take care of his burial.

There was much more to this story that dealt with how I, actually within a few hours after Christopher's death, managed to get not only one portable oxygen cylinder, but two! The generous donor said I needed a spare.   He would not charge me and said they were gifts.

Ah, yes, I shall indeed, 'never forget this as long as I live'. I am humbled, I am grateful, and I pray I shall continue to learn from that 1941 message of "the harried citizen who is pulled one way by "Mystery" and the other by "matter of fact". I am honored to be in the midst of it all.

...that there is help for those who hope...

Chapter 9

THE MOST PERSONAL IS THE MOST UNIVERSAL

It is said the most personal is the most universal. I find that to be so very true in Haiti. Love, sadness, grief, illness and death are experienced in the same way by people everywhere. It is just compounded there by the terrible injustice, the extreme poverty, and the sometimes desperation felt by the people. I have spent time with the poorest of the poor. I feel their pain. I so much want to help them.

During my stays there I have awakened to admire the sound of a rooster crowing. I have heard the mournful wail of mothers' whose precious babies died during the night. In silence I have held, loved, prayed for, and yes, also wailed, when the precious baby has died in my arms.

It is said that the most personal is the most universal. I find that to be so very true in Haiti. Sometimes when I share these stories at home, people will say "Well, it takes a special person to do that". I am not sure about how special I am. Goodness, I have only been doing it since 2008. Father Rick has been there for twenty plus years. He went there as a priest, saw the medical need, came back to the United States to become a physician, and returned to Haiti as both priest and physician. He has started numerous hospitals. He saw the need of many orphans and has built them a true home, a place for them to live where they are taught self-worth and learn that they are loved by the LORD GOD, and by others. They indeed are part of a family.

He saw the sadness of the people who could not afford to bury their loved ones, and had to abandon them. He started Project Tobit. Every week his team literally picks up the bodies from the morgue floor or shelves, prays over them and places them in a proper container for burial in a proper grave forty minutes out of town.

The bodies were originally placed in paper mache coffins. Some still are handled this way, however, the need is so great that it is now necessary to use body bags. Imagine fifteen tiny babies can fit in one body bag. This is repeated over and over again. I know this for a fact, since I have assisted in the loving placement of these little bodies in these bags and have had the honor of placing a rosary with the bodies.

We are not 'bodies with souls', rather we are 'souls with bodies'. When we shed that body, as our soul continues into the next bit of eternal life, the body that encased our soul should be treated with respect and dignity. We should properly e n c a s e it for the burial. And so the need is great for the body bags. I pray for a miracle; actually, I pray for many a miracle, but in this instance I pray that somehow, some company, and some agency, will donate thousands of these body bags to Father Rick, so that the burials

can be done with less worry about having the proper container. Some of the bodies have been in the morgue for a while and are decomposing. Good, heavy, plastic bags are needed!

Last November 2, All Souls Day, I was present at the cemetery along with many Missionaries of Charity (Mother Teresa's sisters) and others, where Father Rick celebrated a beautiful Mass, as he does each year. There was smoke in the mountains, from small fires burning. There were some showers nearby. Father Rick commented how those hills knew the frequent smell of incense, the singing of the hymns, the music of the band, and the prayers that have been repeated over and over again, from his funerals and the burial o f thousands of those dead from the earthquake and cholera epidemic. It was at sunset, the sky really pretty, and we were blessed with not one but two rainbows.

Yes, I do believe the Lord smiled down on us. The band was playing
WHEN THE SAINTS GO MARCHING IN

I actually started to dance with some of the men I know who do the burials each week. We all believe in the RESURRECTION so CELEBRATION seemed just fine. I was so honored to be there.

Chapter 10

I SMELL LIKE DEATH

I smell like DEATH, I know I do! Not of recent death, for sure. This foul stench takes a while to develop. It clings to me. I feel wrapped in it.

I have never actually timed how long I take in the shower, but I know that this is by far the longest I have ever taken. This scrubbing away of DEATH from my body, my hair, takes a long time. I feel badly about using so much precious water here in Haiti, but it is indeed necessary. I know it takes longer than even last week's similar deep cleansing after my time then with DEATH. This seemed to penetrate more. None of the water touches my spirit for that is a different chore for sure!

Today our team once again removed some of the abandoned bodies from the morgue at the General Hospital. They are buried with a proper, respectful funeral outside of town. These bodies today were from the end room of that long, dark, narrow hallway. Is it the first or the last room? I see no numbers. Ah. ALPHA and OMEGA. It is of course a reminder to me of the end of our life on earth and the beginning of the new one in heaven. So, I guess it should be OMEGA and then ALPHA. It is definitely apparent that some of these bodies have been here for a long, long time. Various stages of decomposition are evident. Two that I haven't touched actually look like skeletons. At times, large pieces of skin slough off. At times a hand or a foot comes off as w e pick them up.

And all of this is REALITY. It is not a set design for a horror movie using dummies and harmless chemicals to represent blood and body secretions. Intermittent power outages interfere with the air conditioning units that I see high on the walls. I am not sure just when a generator will kick in, but I recall a recent period of days without much power, resulting in a terrible infestation of maggots. Some bodies are on shelves. Oh, the piles of little babies are so tiny!! Some are wrapped like a piece of meat at a butcher shop. Many are completely naked. Some have clothes on them ...and they seem to be the most difficult for me. One little girl had a colorful head band with a flower on it circling her head. A little boy had on the cutest pair of shorts. They looked so healthy! Others are piled on top of each other on the floor. Once I recall they were waist high. Last week I watched an almost steady pouring of water from these AC units on to the bodies beneath them. These are bodies that had once encased a soul. A soul that came into being by the Life Breath, the Life Energy of our

Loving, Divine, Creator, the Most Generous ONE who shares Himself with us! Now these b o d i e s lie on a smelly, dirty, wet floor. I think of William Shakespeare's comments on 'THE QUALITY OF MERCY', n o t being strained. Droppeth like the gentle rain from heaven upon the place beneath. Well, no way is it gentle, this water that falls and forms puddles on the floor, soaking the clothes of the deceased, and seeming to make the skin macerate even more.

The only thought of MERCY is the prayer that I make.

LORD HAVE MERCY. KYRIE ELEISON.

Yes, Lord, have mercy on those souls who were once in these bodies. Grant them eternal rest. Have mercy on us who do the difficult act of removal and burying, praying all the while...even if it is sometimes just the repeating of the name of JESUS, JESUS, JESUS, over and over. THIS IS NOT AN EASY TASK! Have mercy on all of those who are responsible for leaving them in this condition. Yes, Lord, have mercy and help them find a way to change this awful situation.

No wonder that t h i s shower is taking so long. This touch with DEATH is in my every pore. I once again say, Thank YOU, Lord. There was nowhere else on earth that I would have rather been. AMEN

Chapter 11

HUMILITY

"Just what is it that you learn from your trips to Haiti?" It was a most sincere question by someone I had just met on the airport shuttle from Orlando to Melbourne. Michael had so patiently listened to my sharing of an often overwhelming, intensely extreme, and extremely intense month that I had spent working with Mother Teresa's Missionaries of Charity.

I surprised myself with a rapid response of "OH, OH, how I hope that I can learn **Humility**". It has been some days now since my return and I think of that response, wondering why I did not say to learn COMPASSION. I had very recently studied it for an entire week at a convent in New York. It seemed a bit strange, yet I wonder if my word **Humility**, did not, indeed, include COMPASSION. When I think of **Humility** I consider it a manner of right relationship, knowing just where I stand in relationship to the Creator and to my fellow man. I do not mean a degrading, shameful or mortifying attitude. I would like to have a modest sense of my own "importance", nothing prideful or boastful. I would like to experience life in a patient and compassionate sharing with one another.

In the book 'Compassion' written in 1982 by Macneil, Morrison and Nouwen I learned much about our Compassionate God. I have re-read this book many times, putting my comments in the margins and underlining so much. In it I learn that twelve times in Scripture we see the phrase 'to be moved with compassion'. It is used exclusively in reference to Jesus or His Father. I learned that the Greek word SPLANGCHNIZOMIA reveals the deep and powerful meaning of the expression. The SPLANGCHNA are the entrails of the body, the 'guts'. To the Greek mind they were the place where our most intimate and intense emotions are located. Jesus' compassion was not superficial or fleeting. It extended to the most vulnerable part of His Being.

I smile as I write this because I have been very ill since my return. Severe dehydration from dysentery, metabolic acidosis, and low, low potassium, necessitated a trip to a nearby hospital for fluids and powerful

medication.   It seems that bacteria had entered my body and wanted out,
fast and in a big way.   Ah, yes, a problem with my entrails, my gut.   It is
taking me much longer to recover from this condition.   It does indeed
make me feel more compassion for those in Haiti who have similar
problems; those who might still be living in tents, or on the streets; those
who do not have easy access to a bathroom, or a port-a-potty.   If it was
caused by Cholera many die because they cannot get help in time.   A
friend wondered if I had contracted Cholera.   I had not. It seemed so sad
that I could respond with a "I know the color of cholera".   Of course I
meant that as a nurse. I knew the color and consistency of what a patient
would vomit or expel. It is also sad that, in a way, I do know the 'color of
cholera'. It is often a shade of poverty superimposed on whatever skin
tone the suffering ones have.   Those people who are exposed to the
epidemic, in the middle of the disaster and to the nearness of death.
The sunken eyes that are unforgettable   add darkness to their faces and
to their spirit, whatever, their skin color. It is recognizable even in death.
It is a color I hope I never again have to see.

St Paul wrote to the Colossians (3:12) "You should be clothed in heartfelt
compassion, in kindness and humility, gentleness and patience"   That
surely will make my packing easier, no need for checked attire, Even
way back then it seemed that compassion and humility went together with
patience and kindness as part of the package.

Two recent experiences stand out in my memory of this trip. The first
experience happened on a very hot and seemingly more humid day.   I had
just returned on a crowded 'tap-tap'. These are colorful pick-up trucks
with benches for sitting on each side, in which you tap on the rear window
to tell the driver that it is your stop.   I had been with little Diesel, my
favorite little boy.   He was fifteen months old and suffered from severe
malnutrition.   His skin hung in folds from his floppy body.   He looked
like an old man, Diesel was very ill and we hoped that he could get
admitted to a nearby hospital.   His Aunt Jean was with me.   She is now
his mother since Diesel's mom died during his birth.   There was room at
the hospital but sadly they did not have an in house medical doctor, and did
not know when they would get one. I asked them to take a chest x-ray
please, which they did, since I could pay for it. The clinic doctor   gave me
an unofficial reading of it. It is bad, Pneumonia on top of the tuberculosis.
I knew I had to get him back to the Sisters fast.   I had already given him
the last drop of water from my own water bottle.   Aunt Jean looked
more worried.   We were all tired and sweaty.

I had them wait at an unmanned gate to the Sisters' compound while I went

in haste down to the main entrance with the gateman on duty. I literally 'went down in haste'.

I lost my footing and slid with a few rough bumps that hurt my butt and left me with a scraped, bleeding left foot. The road there is a bunch of pebbles, rocks, rubble of stones and broken bricks that were once part of buildings. **OUCH and OUCH.**

There were four women at the gate needing help of some sort. It is a daily occurrence. The Sisters meet many needs. When the women saw what had happened they did not think twice about helping me. They seemingly forgot their need and rushed toward me. They picked me up. They shook off all that white powdery dust like stuff that gets into one's eyes and irritates mucus membranes. They unstrapped my sandals, shaking out all the little pebbles, and then they put them back on me. They even wiped the blood with their bare hands to remove any foreign object that could have gotten in there. These wonderful women did not speak English. My Creole is pathetically poor, just words or short phrases. Fortunately, I know how to say thanks. I told them MESI ANPIL,

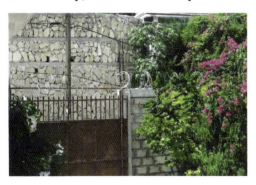

ZANMI MWEM, MESI ANPIL, thanks a lot my friend, thanks a lot. A smile, deep gratitude and prayer were all I had.

After the main gate was unlocked I once more 'went in haste' up the hill to get help for my little Diesel. I cleaned my abrasions as best I could with soap, water, and alcohol...OUCH again. The bit of my blood that I left in the road was a pleasant thought that a little bit of ME would always be in the Haiti that I love so much. In no time at all Sister had an IV going and Rocephin, a potent antibiotic, was in his bloodstream (God bless her skill)!

I prayed for Diesel, his aunt, and the wonderful women at the gate. I asked Mary, the Mother of Jesus, about when she went 'in haste' to help her cousin that she had not seemed to have been hurt. (I recall how when the Beatle, John Lennon, had found himself in times of trouble that he would hear the words of wisdom from Mother Mary. 'There will be an answer, 'Let it be, let it be' If he could hear these words, it came as no surprise to me to hear what I believe she told me.

'I HAD A SURE-FOOTED DONKEY AT MY DISPOSAL. I RODE HIM.

IN THE FUTURE, IF YOU DO NOT SEE A DONKEY, A SURE FOOTED ONE AT THAT, AND KNOW THAT HE IS FOR YOUR PERSONAL USE, FORGET THE WORD HASTE"

It seems that I was to slow down and pay attention. I was not to worry about where I stood in life, rather, in moments like this that I was to worry about where I would place my next footstep. Apparently **Humility** has a commonsense approach to it

The second memory took place at San Fil, another of the Sisters' compounds. .It is known as the House for the Destitute and the Dying. I had been there before and recalled how the women had loved getting a massage. I brought extra lotion in case the Sisters were running low. School was out for the summer and some 400 students were enjoying summer outside activities. It is a large place with separate floors for men and women. I went to a forty bed ward with cots very low to the floor. It makes bending over extremely difficult so I usually sit on the bed with the patient, or kneel on the floor. Most of them have AIDS, TB or a combination of both. By the time they get here they are usually ill unto death. A few were ambulatory, heading for the showers ever so slowly. Most were recumbent.

The first woman I approached looked like a skeleton with a thin layer of tissue stretched over it. I felt like I was massaging bones and only bones. Another just seemed to stare into the air. She apparently wanted my touch. She turned over and extended the other hand, but she just stared into some other world. The base of one woman's neck was covered with some types of growth under the skin. I did not know what they were, perhaps fatty tumors or the beginning of cysts? She placed my hand on them, so I was more than gentle with her giving more of a caress, wanting to soothe her, not hurt her. One young lady was blind in one eye and had frequent and severe coughing spasms that would interrupt the massage. Perhaps I was loosening up some of the lung secretions. She eventually dozed off. One older woman, .probably younger than I, actually did fall asleep while I rubbed her thin body. A younger woman, probably in her twenties, burst into tears as I neared the end of the massage. I wondered if I had somehow hurt her. Of all the women, she was the only one wearing a bra which I thought strange but I did not dwell on that. Many of the other women came rushing over to her cot. Oh the frustration of not knowing Creole. How could I have not made that a priority, a top priority in my life? I knew it was something sad about a baby. Yet I could not tell if the baby had died or could just not be here for some reason. I think that her breasts had milk for the baby. The women seemed to touch her, stroke her individually and as a group. I joined in that ritual type of caring and I held her tightly and silently until the crying stopped.

And then, of course, I always seem to meet a young girl when I am there. Perhaps she is an angel waiting for me. She had been watching me all morning long. When she got closer and noticed the 'starting to scab over' wound on my left foot, she removed my sandals, put my legs up on the cot with a patient and grabbed the lotion. The patient whose bed I shared laughed as her feet were in my face, and mine were in hers. Ah, that spill down the hill once again has women fussing over me. The young teen was ever so gentle with the abrasion, and surprisingly strong on the foot massage. It felt good. Maybe they learn to do that because of all the walking they must do in their routine Haitian life. She then tried on my sandals and paraded around the ward showing everybody. As I lay on that cot I thought how natural it all felt, just like a sleep-over, a pajama party of a sort. I felt closely connected with these women who were strangers to me. I had shared, if only briefly, a part of their lives, the hurting part, the dying part. We shared tears and we made room for laughter.

If I cannot learn *Humility* here in Haiti I am in big trouble. I felt the attention of some women who were indeed 'moved with compassion'. I am deeply grateful to the Lord Jesus, the Ultimate One, who is meek and humble of heart, and compassionate. He has done a great job of 'show and tell'. I look forward to learning more from Him. I found out I have an acute fracture of my tailbone from that spill down the hill. Now I am even just a bit broken like so many of the Haitians. I am broken like the ground, the buildings and many of its people.

I recall ending one of these trip reflections with the thought that perhaps BROKEN was not a bad thing. I do like the idea of being a broken person helping another broken one. It was usually meant in an emotional or spiritual manner. Now I add physical to that.

In that writing I quoted Arthur H. Stainback:

**THE VALUE OF COMPASSION CANNOT BE OVEREMPHASIZED.
NO GREATER BURDEN CAN BE BORNE BY AN INDIVIDUAL THAN TO KNOW THAT NO ONE CARES OR UNDERSTANDS.**

I am trying my best to learn *Humility* and Compassion. I thank Haiti, particularly the women of Haiti, for helping me learn *Humility.*

Chapter 12

COMPASSION

Ah, this compassion directive from the LORD is no easy thing. I do remember that it was meant to be felt all the way down into one's entrails, one's guts. Well, my gut feels it but even more so does my whole being.

In the past 24 hrs I have dealt with much sadness.

I visited Cite Soleil Community School which is run by a friend of mine.

The youngest students were tearing some colored tissue paper into little pieces and then gluing the pieces onto pictures of houses in their coloring book.

I smiled at the blue that each had put on to the roof. Of course that is the color of so many roofs here, blue tarp after blue tarp after blue tarp. Even I, living in a manufactured home in Florida, have had a blue tarp roof after the hurricanes of 2004.

The children were happy to see me and sang a song about Papillion.. ....Butterfly ....just for me.

The upper class was studying the anatomy of the heart, a healthy one.

My heart was a bit sick and heavy as I realized that I would not be needed to help out in the kitchen as I usually do, peeling potatoes, dicing vegetables. There would not be any food for them that day. People in the United States and elsewhere are also in financial binds and many donations are much less.

The lunch time hot meal used to be five days a week, and then cut to three, and now, sadly, only two days. This was not one of those days. Even their hunger for knowledge has been affected since two teachers had to be let go, no funds to pay them.

There has been much violence here in this largest slum in the Western Hemisphere. Fifty people have been killed this week alone. The gangs are feeling a need for revenge, and killing seems to be the only answer. Yes, a real and present danger exists here. Things seem quiet today and I am not afraid. Another friend of mine, a priest who is also a medical doctor tried to be an agent of PEACE, a mediator with both sides of the gangs. As it turned out he was then accused of wrong-doing and had to be interrogated by the local police. This is always a scary experience. In this foreign land, words can get easily twisted. Fortunately, all will be well with him and even more fortunately he has indeed, "smelled the rat". One must be vigilant at all times...

University students have been protesting. One student was shot and died. Many students blame even the United Nation forces. The roads this morning had many obstacles of heavy stones, boulders, blocking access. We had to detour many times. There are many, many uniformed police at intersections. Some streets have less people than usual on them, perhaps they stay at home. I wonder if I am over-reacting now thinking of the calm before a storm. So many people are without work, without food. If an opportunity for work arises, oftentimes a hungry, weakened person is not able to do the job well and is once more let go. People are getting desperate. Desperate people do desperate things. I worry! I worry!

Of course the trip to the Morgue at the General Hospital is always so sad! I am so grateful that Fr. Rick and his team do such a task of love each week. Again, I thank the LORD for allowing me to be there assisting in the praying, the singing, the placing of the dead in body bags. Somehow the bundling of up to fifteen little babies in one body bag always brings tears to my eyes. Many are naked, some with diapers on or other clothes and some wrapped like a piece of meat from the butcher. The hand sewn cloth and the handmade rosaries that are placed in with them seem to bring softness to the horror of it all. Once again, in deep gratitude, I am humbled and honored to say to HIM...'there is no place else that I would rather be'.

Other sadness comes to mind. I have held a two and a half year old little boy in my arms recently. His entire body was covered with scars from being beaten, whipped, hurt badly! Oh, how my heart ached again. The way that I

pray is totally different when I am in Haiti. Sometimes it is merely a long sigh that I know the LORD understands.

It is all I can manage at times. But when I was holding this precious child I rambled out all sorts of 'PLEASE LORD' requests.

PLEASE LET HIM FORGET THE PAIN.

PLEASE LET HIM NOT BE TERRIFIED EACH TIME HE SEES THE ONE WHO DID THIS TO HIM. WAITING AND WONDERING.....

PLEASE LET HIM NOT HAVE TO EXPLAIN ALL THOSE SCARS AS HE GETS OLDER AND HAS TO RELIVE THE PAIN.

PLEASE LET HIM FEEL MY LOVE FOR A BRIEF MOMENT OR TWO.

PLEASE LET HIM KNOW THAT YOU LOVE HIM SO VERY MUCH - AND LET HIM SMILE!

I had a spiritual 'flight' of a sort as I held him close. I envisioned Jesus during His Passion and thought of how His back would have looked during the Scourging. His wounds would be open, and bleeding, and have torn, jagged flesh. I honestly felt that I was embracing Jesus just as I embraced this little boy. I so much want to comfort the Body of Christ, now in Haiti, and in a crazy way, even almost two thousand years ago in Jerusalem.

In **TESTAMENT OF DEVOTION** by Thomas R. Kelly, a Quaker missionary, educator, writer and scholar I learn much. Oh I wish he had not died the year before I was born. I would have so loved to study with him, to pray with him. He shares an instruction on how we are to react to the world, and the way in which we are to respond to our GOD LIGHT within us.

"HE PLUCKS THE WORLD OUT OF OUR HEART, LOOSENING THE CHAINS OF ATTACHMENT. AND HE HURLS THE WORLD INTO OUR HEARTS WHERE HE AND WE TOGETHER CARRY IT IN INFINITELY TENDER LOVE"

Oh my! I am well aware of the plucking that a little bird does to preen itself and get rid of unwanted, non-useful feathers. I want this help from the LORD. I thank Him for doing the plucking of attachment one at a time because I am so not humble enough to give up all, and particularly all at once. I am just too selfish. Even more so am I aware of that hurling. As in times at the morgue, the bit of the world is a real horror. How could such horror be gently placed, anywhere? I am afraid that I might say, "Yes, LORD, I shall carry the world with You with tender love, but I would like to skip the horror part." I am afraid I would say, "No, no...not for me, LORD, for I fear that I am not brave enough." Yet He treats me as He knows me. He hurls it to me--all of the world, the easy part and the hard part! He fills the void that is left after all that plucking. So, with His Love, Grace, and constant Blessing, I can handle what He gives me. I can share in the suffering with those who are hurting wherever in the world He sends me. I learn more about this compassion every day and I hear His whisper that He feels it with me...and not to forget that. We are in this together so to speak.

In the response to the GOD LIGHT within I learn from him that "the basic response of the soul to the Light is internal adoration and joy, thanksgiving and worship, self-surrender and listening. In brief intervals of overpowering visitation we are able to carry the sanctuary frame of mind out into the world, into its turmoil and fitfulness. Continuously renewed immediacy, not receding memory of the Divine Touch, lies at the base of religious living. We must be deadly earnest in our dedication to the LIGHT and be willing to pass out of the first stages, into mature religious living. Only if this is possible can the light from the inner sanctuary of the soul be a workaday light for the marketplace, a guide for perplexed feet, a Recreator of culture patterns for the race of men".

None of this is news to me of course, but I love how his words seem to fit into my life while I am in Haiti, and yes, even here at home dealing with hungry, hurting, homeless, and dying people. I need His gentle prodding not to give up, not to give in and not to let anyone steal my Light. So, I shall just endeavor to stay real close to the LORD, returning often to my inner sanctuary even when I am in the midst of chaos and suffering.

As I leave Haiti now, I once again dare to remind the LORD of the HUNGERS for food, for work, for peace, for education, for healthy bodies, and for clean water. I ask Him to fill these needs, these gnawing hungers. I ask Him first and foremost to fill their hunger for Him and make that hunger greater than all the rest. It is truly the most important hunger in the world.

Chapter 13

LET US CONSPIRE

CONSPIRE, from the Latin, means TO BREATHE TOGETHER. This was the definition way back in the early 1300's, but somehow it took a sinister turn around 1909 and a different meaning of '**agreeing together to do something wrong, illegal, or evil'. I invite you to BREATHE WITH ME!** Eastern spirituality and meditation practices teach us about a focus that is of so much more than just taking in oxygen and releasing carbon dioxide.   They teach us AWARENESS of each breath yes, but also AWARENESS of the very space around us. I have tried to let this be more than a sitting alone in a quiet room experience. I so want this BREATHING and AWARENESS to truly be a part of my everyday life, to help me be attentive.

As I reflect on this current trip of mine to Haiti, I attempt once again to share what MY experiences are like. I cannot answer the profound, the political, and the economic questions.   Wiser ones than I can attempt this thought. I just invite you to CONSPIRE...to BREATHE TOGETHER with me, to become AWARE with me. I am grateful that my own inspiration somehow seems a bit deeper each time. My awareness is a bit more finely tuned and I see more vividly.

The highlight of this trip was the opening of the Malnutrition Center at Mother Teresa's Missionaries of Charity place in Port-au-Prince. It will save the lives of so many babies! I had known the original building before the quake, sitting often in a rocker with little ones in my lap. Last year I had been present as the first shovel entered the earth to start this building.   Now I was part of the many preparations of painting cribs, moving them, applying new and colorful sheets to the fresh mattresses, setting up the medication room, organizing the assessment area, and of course the actual move of the eighty five little babies into the new, bright, cheery and safe building. What a parade that was! Most of them were crying, unsure of what was happening but they soon settled in to the new surroundings. We now even have solar panels for the lighting, no more needing the solar powered lanterns, or a generator. We are harnessing the sun's energy and power to help us see. Just as we always have relied on the Son, the Christ, the Light of the World for our true vision.

There is a bit of routine to my Haiti visits with specific times and places of prayer, helping out at the general clinic and the wound clinics downtown, and assisting at the burials of abandoned bodies at the General Hospital's

Morgue. Of course, this is in addition to the daily routine of the many feedings, holding/loving the b a b i e s , and many a diaper change. Something special and very personal happened to me at each of these times. A few years ago I recall s t u d y i n g /praying on the Scripture passage in Mark 10:46-52. I placed myself in the position of Bartimeus, the blind man calling out for help. And when Jesus asked me: "What do you want me to do for you?" I recall mumbling, " I do not know. I really do not know! Just SURPRISE ME!" Well, the All Powerful, the All Knowing, the All Loving Jesus s u r e has surprised me over and over again with things that only He and I would know about. What a great and personal Jesus we love. I think it is sad that w e do not seem to share the special graces and blessings we receive with others. For a while I too was hesitant, too a f r a i d to verbalize what had happened in my life. Now I think that aging has given me the courage to share.

On a recent trip to the downtown wound clinic a volunteer from France teased me that I reminded her of the Pope as I sat in the front seat of the SUV waving, smiling and blessing the people through the open window. Marie had just s e e n him last year. I quickly assured her that I had no papal or even priestly power to bless anyone. I wanted her to know though, and I did share with her, what my practicing of true B R E A T H I N G and AWARENESS were about. I shared that I wanted all the people I saw, many of whom also waved and smiled, to be aware that I was looking directly a t them. I wanted them to know somehow that t h e y were not 'lost in the crowd', or invisible, or dismissed. I thought of Jesus thousands of years ago having pity on the multitudes. I am sure He is still feeling that way. My heart breaks as I see their poverty, their needs. I too have pity. I realized h o w Jesus performed His miracles on one person at a time. So, I try to also give them a bit of a 'one-on-one' relationship, looking at them individually and fully concentrating o n the one person in front of me. Hopefully they can feel that a fellow traveler in life is aware of their presence. They do not know how much I intercede for them, but the A l m i g h t y does, so perhaps it is 'a blessing' of a sort.

I frequently ride on the back of a motorbike gaining a much closer contact with the people. I get a better view of their awful living conditions. So many people are still in tents t h a t a r e showing the wear and the tear o f two and one half years in the sun, rain and wind. The tents a r e mended with duct tape, corrugated metal pieces, planks of wood and of course, blue tarps.

I live in Florida and have been personally affected by disastrous hurricanes. I well know about blue tarps as a roof and many, many days without p o w e r. But it was a brief span for me, not years. There are so very many people living so close together. The space between the tents, a makeshift alley-way is barely 24 inches, not a chance for a quiet moment there.

I pass sellers of fruits, vegetables, lots of clothing, sunglasses, soaps, plastic basins, sodas like Coke and Sprite, and little bags of drinking w a t e r. Most of the people are right out in the sun, others use the space under

abandoned buses, have tarps or cloth as protection, even umbrellas.

Some are there all day and barely earn enough to feed their family.

Many people carry such heavy and awkward l o a d s on their heads or push them i n a wheelbarrow. Headaches, neck pain, sore backs must be part of their daily lives. The sight that always bothers me most is when I see a man pulling a large, wooden, two-wheeled carrier that contains an extremely heavy load. Often it is many bundles of cloth that surround something, maybe more clothes, I really do not know. But I know it is heavy. I see the well-muscled man straining as he pulls it, occasionally with someone giving a push from behind.

In America I envision a team of oxen pulling this burden. I asked the name of the cart and was told 'brouette'. At first I thought t h e y said 'brutal'. I do believe that I am closer to what it should be called. Oh, how he must hurt at night and all the others who do the same job. I look at all these people in tents, in markets, on the streets, everywhere and I recall the statement of St. Augustine:

"HE LOVES EACH ONE OF US
AS IF THERE WERE ONLY ONE OF US"

Oh, dear Lord, please make their burdens lighter; please heal their aches, pains, hurts, and their worries. Shelter them from too much sun, and the annoying flies and mosquitoes. Send angels to spread their w i n g s to provide a comfortable shady spot, and strong angels to help them pull and push heavy loads. Please keep reminding them of how much you love them.

On Fridays and Sundays, the Sisters open the gate to the outdoor chapel where some local people come faithfully to pray and worship the LORD for one hour. Many of these Haitian people kneel on the bare concrete floor. I do better sitting on a bench with a pole I can lean on for support. I love being with them, even though prayers are in Creole and I do not know all that they are praying. There is just a palpable feeling of belonging for me as I sit there with them. I feel connected to them, part of the Family of Man. I was a bit distracted the other day and kept looking at their feet, covered with calluses and with white chalky dust and dirt. How far did they have to walk to get here? The roads outside the gate are still masses of rubble, concrete and stones galore. The white chalky dust swirls as cars and motorbikes go by. Reconstruction of the building across the street adds to the mess, but is a hopeful sign. I think of Jesus at the Last Supper with basin and towel, washing the feet of the apostles. Oh, how I would love to do that for these people.

A few days later, at the wound clinic, a woman approached Sister. She was about thirty, wearing a short-sleeved navy blue summer dress with a once white collar. It buttoned all the way down the front. On her left foot she had a pink sock with the bottom so covered in real black dirt that it looked like leather--about an inch of it! The right foot was bare and very much swollen. It was why she had come, needing some pain pills. Sister said that she literally lived on the streets--not even in a tent or abandoned building. Sister said she drank a lot and fell, and that is how she hurt her foot. It was not a cut, so pain pills would do. I told Sister I thought I also would drink a lot if I had to live on these streets. She also had some skin condition that was the result of being dirty all the time. I asked Sister if I could give her a bath. I think Sister thought I was joking.

I found a narrow alleyway with no-one in it. The buildings have a concrete bench that is sort of built in, so my lady had a seat. I found a pink plastic basin like I have at home in the Florida hospitals, some surgical soap, and lots and lots of gauze. No washcloths or towels here, but I would do just fine with the gauze. At first she was not sure of me, but then she slowly started to open more and more buttons, as I scrubbed her face, her neck, her upper chest, her back. I had also found some sweet smelling lotion and gave her a nice massage. I am an old fashioned nurse, used to giving many a back rub, so this all felt just fine to me. When I got to her feet, I soaked each one individually for a long time, then pulled the gauze between those dirt encrusted toes, many a time until she was really clean. I was smiling inside wondering just how dirty the apostles' feet were. I do honestly believe that I had a more difficult chore than Jesus did that night. After, I went to Sister to see if she had any socks. Of course my lady did not have any money, so I asked Sister to please look for some emergency money that Sisters usually have for the needs of the poor. I told her I would reimburse her later, and to please ask someone to go into the market area for socks. My lady was most pleased as I managed to get the socks on--even over the swelling. Shoes would have to wait for another time. She smiled at me and thanked me. I smiled and oh, how I thanked the LORD for hearing my desire in that outdoor chapel, knowing what it meant to me, and allowing me not only to wash someone's feet, but almost give them a complete bath. Ah my cup of joy runneth over. What a wonderful SURPRISE from my Jesus.

The Sunday after the Grand Opening was a special day for the fourth graders at the school the Sisters also run. School stops at the fourth grade at the Sisters' school, so they then must go to another place. The church service was in thanksgiving for all they had learned from the Sisters. Of course, it was all in Creole. But oh, how SURPRISED w a s I to hear them singing the entrance song. I did not know the words, but there was no doubt with the melody. It was and is one of my very favorite songs. I am sure it meant much to them, but it meant so much more to me. I sing it to my dying patients many times at the Hospice House where I spend ten hours a week, Often it is the last thing a patient will hear before they die. So, that was most special indeed. The song is YOU ARE MINE by David Haas. I actually had the privilege of hearing him sing it in April and told him about my singing it to the dying. He cried and we shared a long hug. So this was no little thing for me to hear it on that hot, humid, Haiti Sunday.

YOU ARE MINE

I will come to you in the silence.
I will lift you from all your fear.
You will hear my voice,
I claim you as my choice
Be still and know I am here.
Do not be afraid, I am with you
I have called you each by name,
Come and follow me,
I will bring you home
I love you and you are mine.

And then we had a visit to the morgue.

Before we entered the morgue I had seen a deceased person being pushed in a wheelchair, with a bright yellow towel or sheet over their head. I said a prayer for them, knowing that t h e y were from the hospital and the body would soon be placed in a morgue, but just w h e r e I knew not. During the removal of the bodies, I have the honor of placing a rosary in with them. Fr. Rick is praying and blesses each one before we close the body bag. After we had completed all that we could for that day, the team went outside, still singing hymns and praying. I needed to be alone for a bit and so I stayed in that smelly, dark place. I walked down the narrow hall, turned, and in a far corner I saw the yellow towel over a body on the floor. I went and prayed for her, learning now that it was a woman. I told her I was so sorry I did not have any of my rosaries left for her. I turned to leave, and there, on the floor was a ROSARY! It was not at all like the ones I had been distributing. Mine were string/rope knotted ones. This was a multicolored one of beads. Think what you like, but I

59

PROMISE YOU, it is true. It is a small miracle for her and me and a SURPRISE for sure.

I was in a car with my dear friend, Guy, who was driving behind the large truck with the members of the team and Fr Rick, headed for the burial place out of town. I shared with him how very difficult it was to do the removal of the bodies. I mentioned that at times, the only prayer I could do /say/pray was: JESUS, JESUS, JESUS over and over. Guy and I then said it together knowing that it was sufficient and well understood. No sooner had we prayed it, when a very colorful 'tap-tap' drove directly in front of us. On the back, in large and bold letters was the name JESUS.

 And here is a photo of that wonderful affirmation. Another SURPRISE!

On my last day at the center, a f t e r feeding the babies, I asked Sister if she had any construction paper. I needed to make colorful signs with the basic words in English /Creole of the most common things we volunteers n e e d e d. So, I planned on signs for

DIAPER   KOUCHE
FORMULA LET BEBE
WATER/   DLO

These would be right in plain view and make it easy for everyone (workers and volunteers), but I wanted them to match and stand out. School was out, so no one was at the school. Sister thought perhaps I might find some paper in the Depot area, which is a storage place up the hill a bit. There is still construction going on there, and it had the little string roped off areas awaiting a concrete sidewalk. So, there was no luck going that way. I for some reason decided to find another way of getting there. I went down a different walkway turned up the road, saw an open door and heard voices in the room, but not close. There was a chair right at the entranceway that had books piled on it, and on the top of the books was a pack of multi-colored construction paper. OF COURSE THE PAPER WAS THERE!!! WHY DID I DOUBT? I took two pieces, thanked the Lord, and left the spot that I had never ever even been in or seen before. Ah SURPRISE once again.

I shared all of these ramblings with my spiritual director, Father Steve, of course. He gave me a bit of an insight I had not thought about. It goes back to Genesis 12 with the LORD telling Abram to go forth and explaining that He, the LORD will bless him, so that he will be a blessing!

I smiled when the French volunteer, Marie told me I reminded her of the Pope giving blessings. Now I wonder if the LORD does not ask all to leave the place where we are, the safe and sure place to leave our own self, to go and be with others, helping them when we are able. In a way

THE LORD WILL BLESS US TO BE A BLESSING FOR OTHERS.

It is NOT me blessing anyone, but BEING a blessing, because of the power of the Holy One. Even that new way of looking at BLESSINGS was a SURPRISE.

I pray that all who have taken this very long journey with me…who actually did CONSPIRE WITH ME may now be willing to accept that honor also, to BE A BLESSING for others, near and far. May the LORD bless us all! AMEN, AMEN

Chapter 14

THE WHISTLING OF MY FATHER

It is a Wednesday in August and I am again in Haiti. Hundreds of needy people are at the Missionaries of Charity compound awaiting distribution of food. Some are still outside the gate; others are seated in the large area outside my window. It is a chapel for Sunday mass and is open on one side. There are many benches that can hold the 450 students and many others. Those who wait today do not do it silently. It is noisy; very, very noisy.

Amazingly, I hear a bird sing; a song that I am not familiar with in Florida. It rises above the confusion of the crowd. It sings out above them and stands out above the din to me. This surprise reminds me of when I was a little girl. My most practical and loving father had arranged a way for me to find him, if I ever got lost in a crowd, or if for some reason we got separated from each other. It was a special manner of whistling that he did. It was a short melodic piece that he would repeat three times, and then he would do it again as many times as needed. Somehow that sound would rise above the noise of a crowd. All I had to do was follow the sound. It reassured me that he was nearby, even if I could not see him. I followed the sound of the whistling, listening intently, knowing that all would be well and I would soon find him. There was no need to be afraid or to cry. I can recall how he would even whistle it while walking down the street when he came to visit me, if I was staying elsewhere. I would hear that sound, know that he was near and my heart would begin to be happy.

I can still hear that whistle in my mind today. I smile at the very thought of it, and, oh yes, I do cry this time. They are tears of gratitude for that wonderful father, who loved me so much that he even would anticipate the possibility of us being separated and provided a sure way for me to find him. He stayed where he was. I was to follow the sound. How very fortunate I was to have such a father.

I leave that remembering and take joy in knowing that if my earthly father would do that f o r me, our Heavenly Father would do the same. Part of me knows that I have managed to find my way back to Him when I would wander but I would like to remember that secret and special way HE has for me to find Him. I am getting older and do occasionally have senior moments in which I forget a name, or the right word. Eventually I get it, but it takes longer than it should. I pray that as I advance in age I also advance in wisdom. I pray I can always recall that special and secret sound the Heavenly Father has for me. Perhaps, just perhaps, we could substitute it with my father's whistle that I have never forgotten. That way I shall always be able to find HIM, no matter what happens, if I wander away spiritually or physically.

On this day in Haiti He has once again provided me with this wonderful memory for which I am so very grateful. The song of that bird, the whistling by my father, and most especially for our all-loving and wise Father in Heaven who has sent His Son, Jesus to redeem me and all of mankind. This all-knowing Father has time and time again helped me never lose my hearing for that secret and special song that He has for me. I am confident that if I should, He will show me another way to reach HIM.

I thank the Lord for that assurance and do hope that the hungry people awaiting the food will be blessed with the song of that little bird I heard, and always be able to find their way back to Him also. Thank You, Amen

Chapter 15

OUTER SPACE—INNER SPACE

The area in which I live is called the "SPACE COAST". Space is a familiar term and concept for many of us who live here. It affects our lives from the areas of employment to personal goals, to our very dreams. Shuttle launches into the great beyond became almost a routine occurrence.

Today I consider the word SPACE in another manner, still mysterious and taking me into an unknown territory. Years ago I used to bring my Aunt Edna to church each week. We would get there early so that she could get her favorite pew in the large and often crowded church. I would sit in that pew also, but not real close to her. I tried to tell her that I needed my space. She replied, "No dear, you DEMAND your space"! I had not realized it in that way, yet it was true. I most definitely did not feel comfortable being so close to some people. Edna was not my favorite aunt by any means so there was always a bit of distance in our relationship and even in our church pew. In looking up that term "personal space", I find that it is a psychological term which describes a certain amount of inches around us that we consider 'ours' and we do not let just anyone into that safe, protected place. We reserve the spot closest to us for our more intimate relationships and giving the space farthest away for strangers. I still do that.

I have just returned from another trip to Haiti. I smile, realizing that I am so very different when I am there. Many, many people attend the church services there. We sit on long wooden benches that are very close together, not much leg room there. Oh, how close together the people sit. Yet this does not bother me at all. Sometimes I know the people, most often I do not, but we squeeze together, always somehow finding room for another. I fit right in! It does not matter that I am older, white skinned, and American. Funny, the Haitian people seem to not know anything about this psychological concept of personal space. Even in their daily transport in tap-taps, everyone squeezes in, carrying everything from products bought or to sell at the market, including chickens, dead or alive!

The church service is in Creole and the priest always gives long sermons. Even though I might know the Scripture readings for that day, I have no real idea what he is teaching us. So, once again I wander in my imagination, my personal prayer. I have been very much concentrating on a type of prayer called CONTEMPLATION. I believe it will be a lifetime project until I get it right. Years ago Fr. Walter Burghardt, SJ described it as 'A LONG LOVING LOOK AT THE REAL' I loved that idea and strive always to be more aware and attentive, trying to glean what REAL truly is.!

Recently I came across another definition by Fr. Ronald Rolheiser. For him CONTEMPLATION is 'TO LIVE ONE'S LIFE IN SUCH A WAY AS TO MAKE A SPACE FOR GOD TO ENTER IN AND TO LET GOD BE GOD:' Now my reflections on SPACE have a different aim. I must learn to make space for God to enter in. I must empty my soul of the clutter of worldly concerns and constant noise. I wish to give him a space, a place filled with silent yearning, awaiting His coming in Faith. Of course, I know that I do have God's presence in me. I would not be here without that. But this PRESENCE is of a different kind, a more knowing type, that will help me to be truly alive to the needs of those around me, the ones I sit comfortably close to as we touch bodies, touch spirits, and also to those whom I have kept at a distance, not wanting them into "my" private, personal space. I am confident that HE will teach me how to do this.

My outer space and my inner space both seem to blend, as I yearn and as I learn to travel in a territory that is a bit unknown, often scary. I need no spaceship or shuttle. I pray that I may truly learn to take long, loving looks at the real, and blend that with living a life of Faith, Hope and mostly LOVE. My means of transport will be God HIMSELF, carrying me where I need to be. Living on the 'SPACE COAST' is fine. For me I shall just make it GOD'S SPACE COAST.

Chapter 16

NOT *QUITE* A CONCLUSION

The dictionary would say a conclusion is a "final part of something", the "part that brings something to a close". I could not possibly think that this would be a conclusion of what Haiti is for and to me. HAITI, the word itself, means LAND OF HIGH MOUNTAINS, and has much to accomplish, as do I.

Sometimes when I look at those mountains I feel that they have a double meaning. I envision many a 'mountain ' of problems right there along with all of nature's beauty. I take the vision even further, thinking of the expression "the elephant in the room" (many a mountain reminds me of that awesome animal, the elephant). That expression is an old metaphor, an idiom for an obvious truth that is either being ignored or going unaddressed. It also applies to something that no one wants to talk about. As I think of that elephant I go to the story, the parable, from ancient India. My favorite WIKIPEDIA search, tells the story.

In various versions of the tale, a group of blind men (or men in the dark) touch an elephant to learn what it is like. Each one feels a different part, but only one part, such as the side or the tusk. They then compare notes and learn that they are in complete disagreement. The stories differ primarily in how the elephant's body parts are described, how violent the conflict becomes and how (or if) the conflict among the men and their perspectives is resolved.

In some versions, they stop talking, start listening and collaborate to 'see' the full elephant. When a sighted man walks by and sees the entire elephant all at once, they also learn that they are blind. While one's subjective experience is true, it may not be the totality of truth. If the sighted man was deaf, he would not hear the elephant bellow. Denying something you cannot perceive ends up becoming an argument for your limitations."

Perhaps, I also am a bit blind, or in the dark with my experience of Haiti. I have by choice mostly dealt with those in a congested, busy city, in Cite Solei, that large and dangerous slum, and with the poor....the poorest of the poor. I know little about the country, the mountain life, even the parts of Haiti that have people who have jobs, nice homes, cars, better than average education. I know very little about the politics, wondering about the rumors of corruption that I hear. I do realize that I need to learn more, to broaden my scope, to move to another part of that elephant. I perhaps, have done an injustice to the Haiti as a whole, the Haiti that I love.

In the areas I have spent my time, I do see rainbows after dark clouds and storms.

I truly had such a fun time on my last visit watching butterflies, and taking photos of them on pretty flowers. They are such a sign of HOPE, new life, new beginning. They had spent time in a cocoon in which they disappeared and appeared to be dead.

Elisabeth Kubler Ross has often spoken of the numerous drawings of butterflies that she saw in the barracks of concentration camps in Europe. Children and adults had scratched them into the wooden walls. Many a Hospice has them for their symbol. The ancient Greek word for butterfly was PSYCHE, meaning SOUL.

I shall hang onto this thought of butterflies all over Haiti, as a sign of new life, new beginnings of HOPE. Many times when I bring gifts to the people, especially the children in that school in Cite Soleii...I bring them in a little blue canvas bag that has **HOPE** in large letters. It reads: " YOU ARE MY HOPE LORD, IN YOU I TRUST, and ON YOU I DEPEND." Psalm 71: 5.

I try to make them aware of the importance of the LORD in their life. Many times, it is they who remind me. I close with the thought of those children in the lowest grade, the PAPILLION group singing to me a few weeks ago... singing of butterflies. I pray that they never lose the

HOPE. I pray that I am able to assist them in the new beginnings of a better life for them, with education, better housing conditions, improved health. and the ability to have something to eat every day. I hope that any CONCLUSION of HAITI would have it for all. There is much to be done. With the help of the LORD, I shall continue to do my little bit helping the person in front of me, one at a time.

AMEN..AMEN

These are Patricia's thoughts when she was asked to reflect upon herself.

Chapter 17

NO LONGER HIDDEN

Hidden object games on the computer fascinate me. I consider myself an observant person so I thought I would excel at doing these mental challenges. Ah, was I in for a surprise! I most definitely needed help. Instead of excelling, I felt very lacking. I needed assistance! I found this assistance by using a MAGNIFYING GLASS! I just could not do it alone.

This MAGNIFYING GLASS, this hand held lens, depends on where it is placed between the viewer and the object. It enlarges the image and helps one focus. Things do not change, just one's perspective, one's vision. Yes it helps one define.

Sometimes I cannot see what I am looking for because of the surrounding clutter. Sometimes I am definitely looking in the wrong place. I need a wider view to look at the whole picture. Sometimes the object has so blended in with the color, the pattern, that it almost seems a part of the picture itself. It is almost indiscernible. Ah, and sometimes I am sure that they have made a terrible mistake - it is not there at all! And then, with the assist of my new friend, that MAGNIFYING GLASS, I see what was there all the time, awaiting my discovery. I smile and am filled with joy.

My mind now jumps to Scripture. Luke 1:46-55 --THE MAGNIFICAT

MY SOUL MAGNIFIES THE LORD

AND MY SPIRIT REJOICES IN GOD MY SAVIOR;

BECAUSE HE HAS REGARDED THE LOWLINESS OF HIS HANDMAID;

FOR BEHOLD, HENCEFORTH ALL GENERATIONS SHALL CALL ME BLESSED.

BECAUSE HE WHO IS MIGHTY HAS DONE GREAT THINGS FOR ME, AND HOLY IS HIS NAME;

AND HIS MERCY IS FROM GENERATION TO GENERATION ON THOSE WHO FEAR HIM,

HE HAS SHOWN MIGHT WITH HIS ARM.
HE HAS SCATTERED THE PROUD IN THE CONCEIT OF THEIR
HEART.

HE HAS PUT DOWN THE MIGHTY FROM THEIR THRONES, AND
HAS EXALTED THE LOWLY.

HE HAS FILLED THE HUNGRY WITH GOOD THINGS,
AND THE RICH HE HAS SENT AWAY EMPTY.

HE HAS GIVEN HELP TO ISRAEL, HIS SERVANT, MINDFUL OF HIS
MERCY

EVEN AS HE SPOKE TO OUR FATHERS, TO ABRAHAM AND TO HIS
POSTERITY FOREVER.

Mary sings to Elizabeth... "My soul magnifies the LORD and my spirit
rejoices in God." Mary knows that GOD has regarded her lowliness and yet
HE used her. Richard Rohr describes the word 'regardez' a French based
word ...that means to 'look at twice, or look at again or look at deeply'. He
describes how Mary allows herself to be looked at with GOD's deeper and
more considered gaze. My mind wanders a bit picturing GOD using a hand
held lens (which I know HE does not need). I ask HIM to look at me again
and deeply. Mary's prayer, her hymn to HIM, gives me much on which to
meditate. Mostly right now it leads me to make a fervent prayer of my own.

Dear Lord, help me to be a MAGNIFYING GLASS, a tool, to help others
who are searching to find you. Help me show others how to see better in the
midst of much clutter, to focus. Help me to show others where to look. Help
me point out that YOU indeed do stand out when they think you have faded
into the background of their lives. Help me to make them aware that no
terrible mistake has been made. YOU are there—always-- all ways-- even
when they think that YOU just cannot be seen--or found. Help them to have
the joy of finding YOU,

In the earlier part of Luke's gospel he describes the visit of the archangel,
Gabriel, telling Mary how she has been chosen to be the human instrument
to bring forth Incarnation. I often pause at the part where---AND THE
ANGEL LEFT. I wonder how Mary dealt with that news when she was all
alone. Well, she apparently did not spend too much time on herself. Luke
says that she 'went in haste' to help Elizabeth and then to sing GOD's praises.

I pray that I might also truly MAGNIFY THE LORD as HIS tool---and go in haste to help others. I am most grateful that GOD has looked twice, looked deeply at me His lowly servant. Indeed HOLY IS HIS NAME...

AMEN...AMEN

ISBN-13: 978-1482365665
Printed in the USA by Amazon Printing. All rights reserved.

This book was compiled and edited by my friend, Gail Pearson, from reflections written after my trips to Haiti.

Made in the USA
Charleston, SC
03 February 2014